A Gift For

❖ FROM ❖

KISSES

a photographic celebration

BOK7000

A kiss is a lovely trick designed by

nature to stop speech when words

become superfluous.

Ingrid Bergman

Happiness is like a kiss –

in order to get any good

out of it you have to give

it to somebody else.

Anonymous

A kiss

a comma, a question mark, or an exclamation point.

Mistinguett (Jeanne Marie Bourgeois)

The sound of a kiss is not so loud as that of a cannon,

but its echo lasts a great deal longer.

Oliver Wendell Holmes

The anatomical juxtaposition of

two orbicularis oris muscles in a

state of contraction.

scientific definition of a kiss, Dr. Henry Gibbons

If you are ever in

doubt as to whether

or not you should

kiss a pretty girl,

always give her the

benefit of the doubt.

Thomas Carlyle

14

It is quite a delight to receive a well-intentioned and

appropriate kiss. Please feel free to make the gesture.

Eleanor Ironside

When women kiss it always reminds

one of prize-fighters shaking hands.

H. L. Mencken

Stolen sweets are always sweeter

Stolen kisses much completer.

Leigh Hunt

Platonic friendship is the interval

between the introduction

and the first kiss.

R. Woods

A pleasant reminder

that two heads are

better than one.

definition of a kiss. Rex Prouty

"Kiss" rhymes to "bliss"

in fact as well as verse.

Lord Byron

Where do the noses go?

I always wondered where

the noses would go.

Ernest Hemingway

If you finally decide to

let a man kiss you, put

your whole heart and

soul into it. No man

likes to kiss a rock.

Lady Chesterfield

How delicious is the winning of a kiss at love

eginning.

omas Campbell

Kissing is a means of getting

two people so close together

that they can't see anything

wrong with each other.

Gene Yasenak

Kissing don't last: cookery do!

George Meredith

To a woman the first kiss is the end of the beginning; to a man it is the beginning of the end.

Helen Rowland

When soul

meets soul on

lovers' lips

Percy Bysshe Shelley

Kissing your hand may make

you feel very very good but a

diamond and sapphire bracelet

lasts for ever.

Anita Loos

It was thy kiss, Love, that made me immortal.

Margaret Witter Fuller

But I wasn't kissing

her. I was whispering

in her mouth.

Chico Marx

He kisses me and now

I am someone else;

someone else in the

pulse that repeats the

pulse of my own veins

and in the breath that

mingles with my breath.

Gabriela Mistral

49

Don't wait to know her better to kiss her;

kiss her, and you'll know her better.

Anonymous

...let us kiss each other's eyes,

And laugh our love away.

William Butler Yeats

Some men kiss and do not tell, some kiss and tell.

Susan Langstaff Mitchell

A kiss is a secret told to the

mouth instead of to the ear.

Edmond Rostand

We are all mortal

until the first kiss

and the second

glass of wine.

Eduardo Galeano

Like dreams the

warmest kisses flee,

Like kisses, soon all

joys are gone.

Johann Wolfgang von Goethe

My first kiss can be

summed up in one

word: unsuccessful.

Huey Lewis

Take me by the

earlaps and match

my little lips to

your little lips.

Plautus

Everyone wants a hug and kiss.

It translates into any language.

Georgette Mosbacher

67

Kisses may not

spread germs,

but they certainly

lower resistance.

Louise Erickson

Never a lip is curved with pain

That can't be kissed into smiles again.

Bret Harte

Kissing power is stronger than will power.

Abigail Van Buren

Kisses are like

confidences –

one follows

the other.

Denis Diderot

After the kiss comes the

impulse to throttle.

Wystan Hugh Auden

76

A thing of no use to one, but prized by two.

Robert Zwickey

Why did you keep

me on tiptoe so

long if you weren't

going to kiss me.

Tom Mathew

A kiss can be even deadlier if you mean it.

from the film "Batman Returns"

Lovers can live on kisses and cool water.

Old French Saying

There are all sorts of

kisses…from the sticky

confection to the kiss of death.

Of them all, the kiss of an

actress is the most unnerving.

how can we tell if she means it

or if she's just practising?

Ruth Gordon

My plan was to kiss her with every lip on my face.

from the film "Dead Men Don't Wear Plaid"

It takes a lot of

experience for a girl to

kiss like a beginner.

from the "Ladies Home Journal", 1948

Giving kisses,

stealing kisses,

Is the world's chief

occupation.

Ludwig Christoph Heinrich Hölty

Kisses are the messengers of love.

Danish Proverb

Wherever one wants to be kissed.

Coco Chanel, on where to wear perfume

That farewell kiss which resembled greeting, that last glance of love which becomes the sharpest pang of sorrow.

George Eliot

You must remember this,

a kiss is still a kiss.

A sigh is just a sigh:

Herman Hupfeld

Picture Credits

cover starting from top left: A couple kissing in an MG Midget sports car, circa 1970; Robert Young and Joan Marsh, two MGM film stars, circa 1931; Romance in Cowaden, Glasgow, UK, 1958; Frances Huggins gets a kiss from her pet dog after coming first in a baby show, 1941; A little boy and girl hold hands on the beach, 1965. Alan Band/Hulton Getty Picture Collection; Two lovers share an unusual bicycle for a romantic trip through Italy, 1947; A couple on honeymoon in Jersey, 1953; A little girl kisses her brother, 1941.

title page: A young girl kissing her teddy bear under the mistletoe, circa 1936.

page 4/5: A couple kiss on Wimbledon Common, UK, 1957.

page 6/7: Two of the stars of Hal Roach's "Our Gang", on Santa Monica beach during filming, circa 1930.

page 8: A couple kissing on a cross-channel trip, 1962.

page 10: A man kisses his wife and daughter goodbye as he sets off to work in Northern Alberta, 1951.

page 13: A laboratory technician watches a couple test the durability of a lipstick, circa 1950.

page 14/15: Robert Young and Joan Marsh, two MGM film stars, circa 1931.

page 17: A boy kisses his Boston terrier, circa 1955.

page 18/19: Miss Egypt is crowned "Miss World", 1954.

page 20: Children share a peck on the cheek, 1981.

page 22: An evening embrace, 1953.

page 24: A courting couple relax in the park, 1951.

page 26/27: A couple in the South of France, 1954.

page 29: Railway porters kiss under mistletoe received for distribution throughout London, UK, 1937.

page 31: A couple kissing in evening dress, circa 1950.

page 33: A little boy and girl hold hands on the beach, 1965. Alan Band/Hulton Getty Picture Collection.

page 35: A couple wearing bubble helmets kissing, circa 1942. Weegee/Hulton Getty Picture Collection.

page 36: Mr and Mrs Townsend celebrate their golden wedding with a kiss, 1939.

page 38: Stuart Erwin and Susan Fleming in the film "He Learned About Women", circa 1932.

page 40/41: Dame Margot Fonteyn and Rudolf Nureyev in "Pelleas and Melisande", Covent Garden, London, UK, 1969.

page 42: A contestant in the "Miss World" competition has her hand kissed by an admirer, 1953.

page 44: One of the Weekiwachee Mermaids performs her "aquaballet" act, Florida, circa 1950.

page 46/47: A scene from the play "Aren't We All?" by Frederick Lonsdale, 1929.

page 48/49: A couple in a motel, England, 1955.

page 51: A couple kissing in Battersea Pleasure Gardens, London, UK, 1951.

page 52/53: Actors Mark Hashfield and Simone Lovell in the South of France for a photo-fiction serial, 1954.

page 55: A couple embrace in an alley, 1945.

page 56: As title page.

page 58/59: A couple kissing by the Seine with Notre Dame Cathedral behind them, Paris, France, 1952.

page 60/61: Grand Central Station, New York, 1958. © Ernst Haas courtesy Hulton Getty Picture Collection.

page 63: A boy kissing Linda the llama, circa 1955.

page 65: A little girl kisses her brother, 1941.

page 66/67: Two walruses kiss at the Hagenbeck Zoo, Hamburg, Germany, 1967.

page 68/69: British troops stationed in Germany fraternise with local girls, 1945.

page 70: A woman greets her son, an Austrian prisoner of war returning home to Vienna, 1947. © Ernst Haas courtesy Hulton Getty Picture Collection.

page 73: Kirk Douglas and Angie Dickinson in the United Artists film "Cast a Giant Shadow", 1965.

page 74/75: Lovers in Notting Hill Gate, London, UK, 1967. David Newell Smith, The Observer/Hulton Getty Picture Collection.

page 76/77: Mary Bolande kisses her co-star Charlie Ruggles in Paramount's "Mama Loves Papa", 1933.

page 78: Romance in Cowaden, Glasgow, UK, 1958.

page 80/81: A keeper at London Zoo receives a kiss from a friendly sea-lion, 1934.

page 82: Hop pickers working at Goudhurst in Kent, UK, escape to a quiet spot for romance, 1949.

page 85: A couple on honeymoon in Jersey, 1953.

page 86: Pupils at the Central School of Drama in London, UK, practise a theatrical kiss, 1954.

page 89: Daniel Massey and his girlfriend Judith Scott, during a break in filming "The Queen's Guards", 1960.

page 91: Two lovers share an unusual bicycle for a romantic trip through Italy, 1947.

page 92/93: A couple embrace by a river, 1952.

page 95: Frances Huggins gets a kiss from her pet dog after coming first in a baby show, 1941.

page 97: A pair of lovers reflected in a scent atomiser, circa 1959. Weegee/Hulton Getty Picture Collection.

page 99: A couple on a transatlantic voyage, 1931.

page 100/101: Ann Todd and Gregory Peck exchange a kiss in a scene from Alfred Hitchcock's "The Paradine Case", 1947.

ISBN: 0-06-18547-3

Library of Congress Cataloging-in-Publication Data

CIP data has been applied for.

Printed in Italy

1 2 3 4 5 6 7 8 9 10

Design: WDA
Text and picture research: Suzie Green
Series Editor: Elizabeth Carr